MY PHONICS WORDS

The Sound of AY

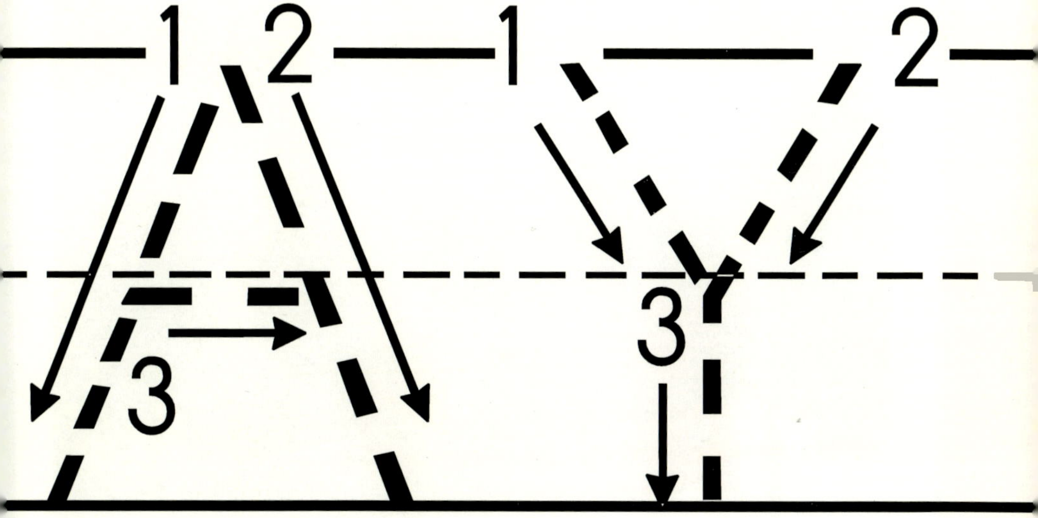

CHRISTINA EARLEY

A Little Honey Book

Crabtree Publishing
crabtreebooks.com

pay

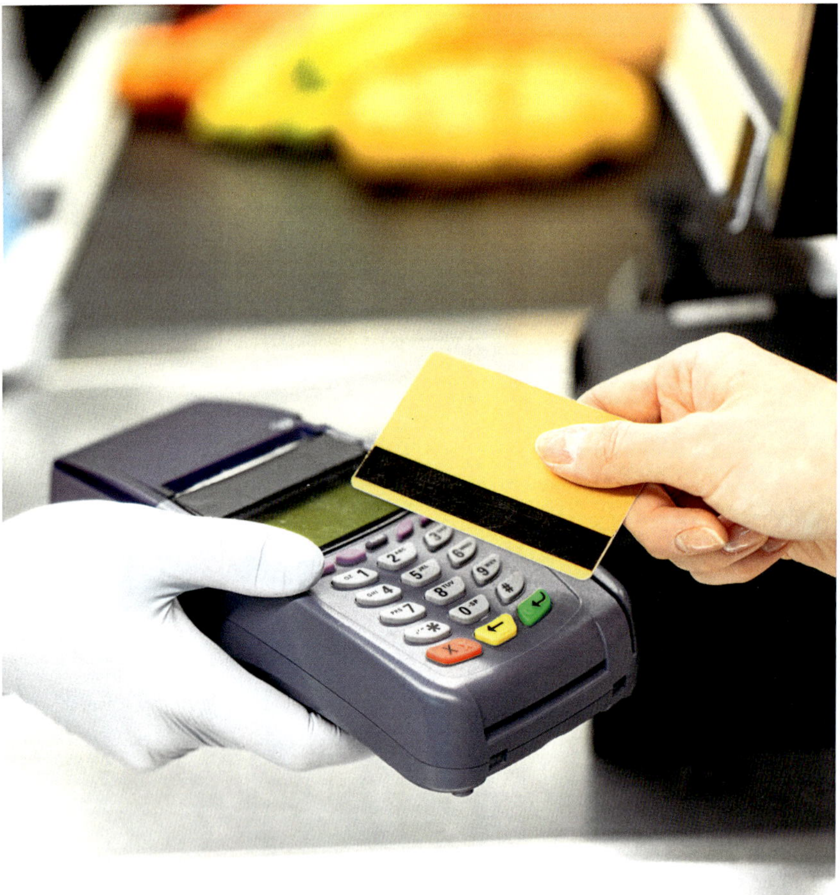

bay

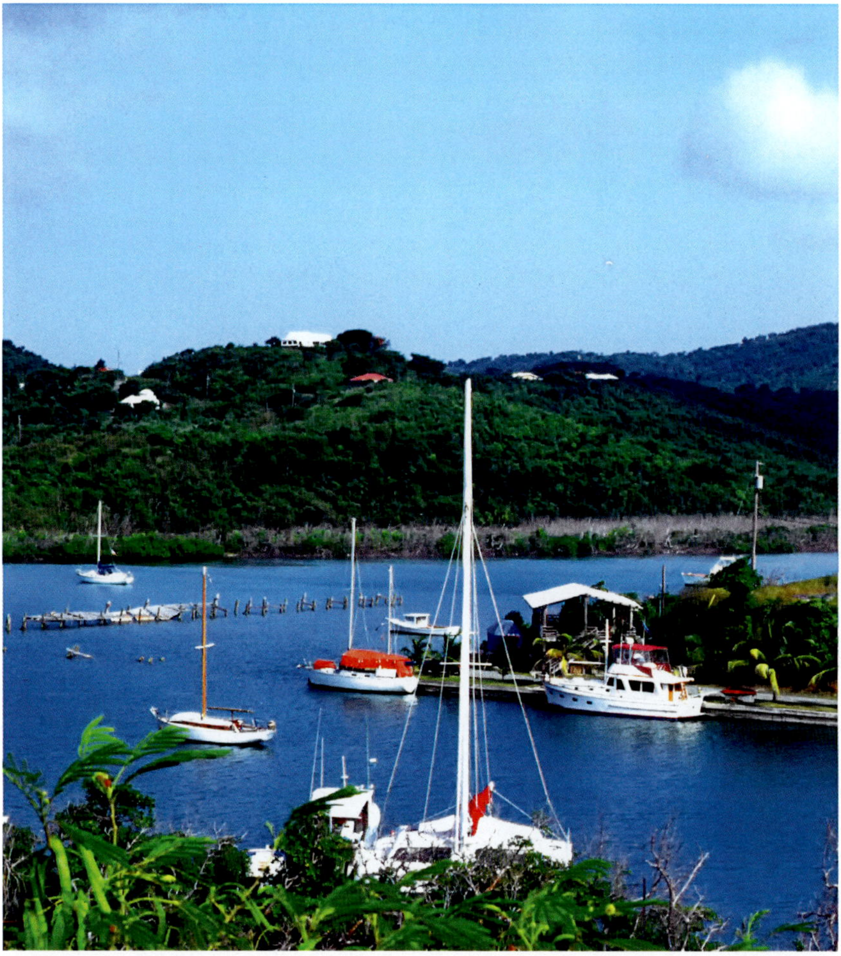

ray

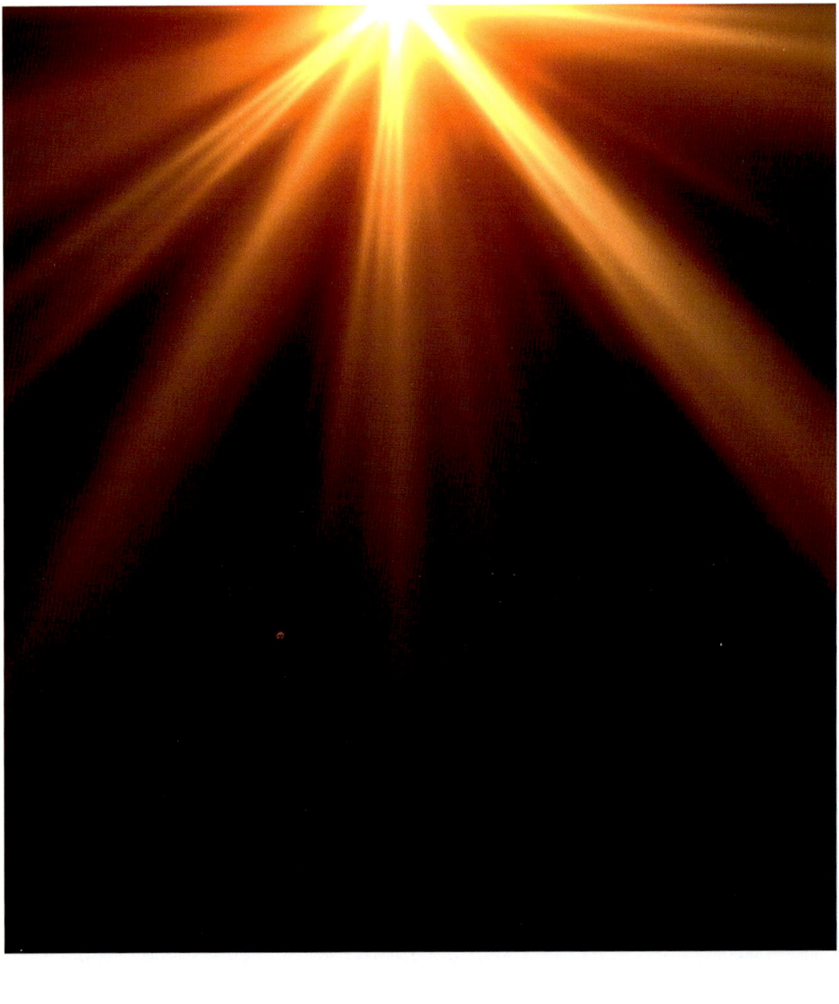

jay

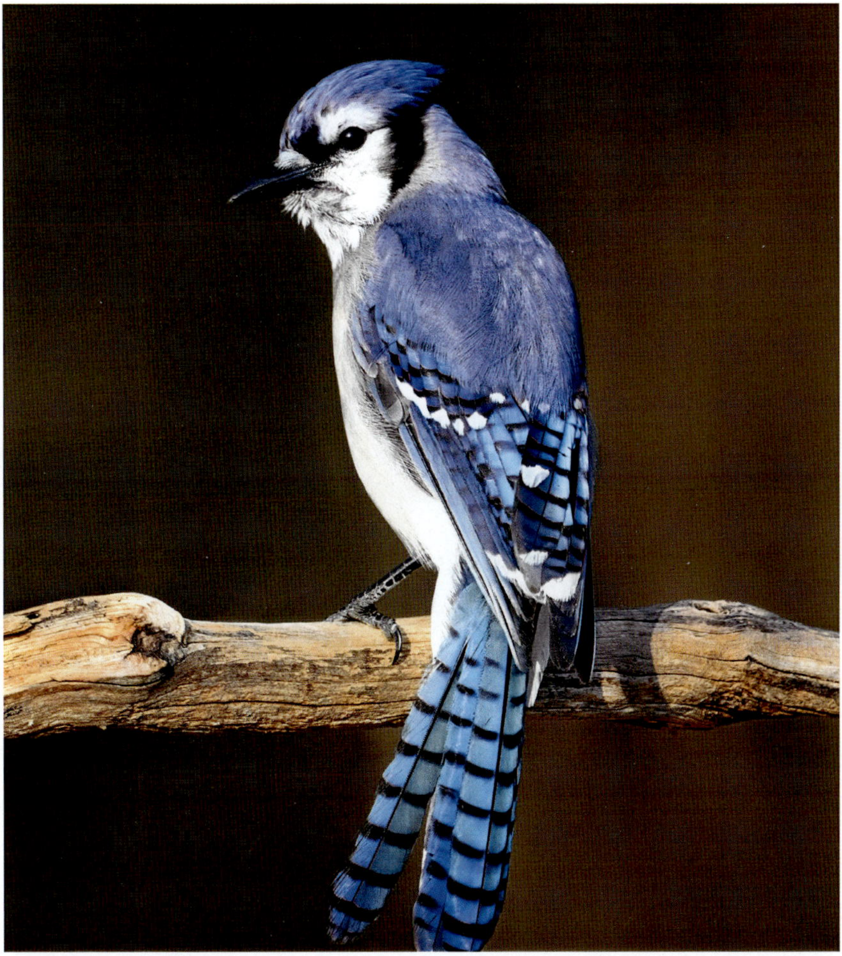

gray

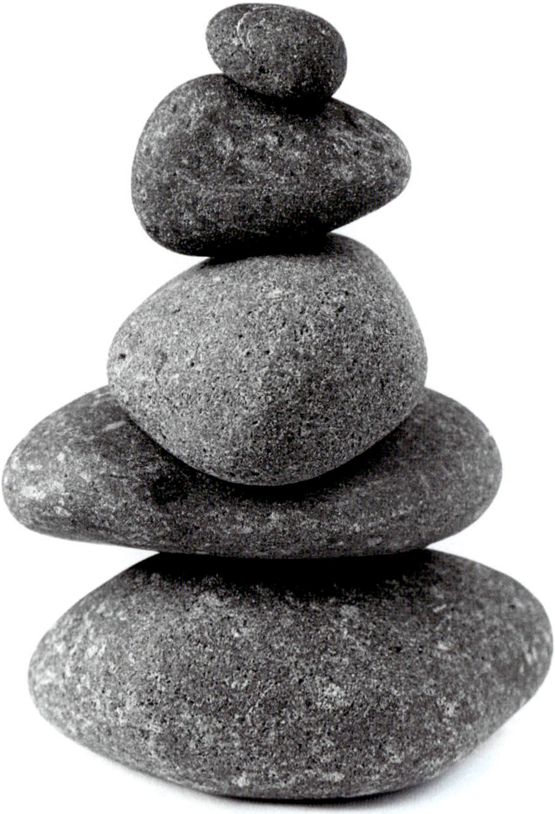